D1736820

The Blacksmith

by Rennay Craats

WEIGL EDUCATIONAL PUBLISHERS

Published by Weigl Educational Publishers Limited
6325-10 Street SE
Calgary, Alberta
Canada T2H 2Z9
Web site: www.weigl.com
Copyright 2004 WEIGL EDUCATIONAL PUBLISHERS LIMITED

Canadian Cataloguing in Publication Data
Craats, Rennay, 1973-
        The blacksmith / Rennay Craats.

(Early Canadian life)
Includes index.
ISBN 1-55388-035-8 (lib. bound: alk. paper)
ISBN 1-55388-053-6 (pbk.)

        1. Blacksmiths--Canada--History--Juvenile literature. 2. Blacksmithing--Canada--History--Juvenile literature. 3. Frontier and pioneer life--Canada--Juvenile literature. I. Title. II. Series: Early Canadian life (Calgary, Alta.)

TT220.C73 2003   j682'.0971   C2003-905434-9

Printed and bound in the United States of America
1 2 3 4 5 6 7 8 9 0 06 05 04 03

We acknowledge the financial support of the Government of Canada through the Book Publishing Industry Development Program (BPIDP) for our publishing activities.

Photograph Credits
Every reasonable effort has been made to trace ownership and to obtain permission to reprint copyright material. The publishers would be pleased to have any errors or omissions brought to their attention so that they may be corrected in subsequent printings.

Ellen Bryan: pages 3T, 12, 13T, 13B, 15T, 15B; **Glenbow Archives:** pages 1 (NA-1260-2), 3B (NA-750-8), 5 (NA-1510-1), 6 (NA-1260-2), 7 (NA-1709-52), 8 (NA-750-8), 9 (NA-3976-13), 15MT (NA-1097-5), 16 (NA-1260-1); **Green Family Forge, Trinity NL:** pages 14T, 20, 23L; **Nova Scotia Museum:** pages 4 (971.621 BL9), 15MB (P270.37), 23B (971.621 BL15); **photocanada.com:** page 10; **photos.com:** pages 11, 18; **Tina Schwartzenberger:** pages 14B, 23R.

Project Coordinator
Tina Schwartzenberger

Design
Janine Vangool

Layout
Bryan Pezzi

Copy Editor
Michelle Lomberg

Photo Researcher
Ellen Bryan

Contents

Introduction

Early settlers often travelled to Canada with few belongings. When they arrived in Canada to start their farms, the settlers often did not have many tools. At that time, there were no hardware stores selling tools. Pioneers had to create the tools they needed. As more settlers arrived and a community grew, blacksmiths often settled in the area.

This blacksmith shop has made horseshoes, nails, and tools since it was established in the 1870s. It is now located in Sherbrooke Village in Nova Scotia.

Without the blacksmith, pioneers would have gone without many important goods and services. By the end of the nineteenth century, most villages had three to five blacksmiths.

For hundreds of years, the blacksmith was an important part of every town. Farmers, shopkeepers, and business owners used the blacksmith's services. Blacksmiths were skilled workers who made and repaired iron and metal tools and other objects. Blacksmiths made cooking utensils, hooks, horseshoes, nails, and tools. They kept carriages and other equipment running well, too. Blacksmiths also repaired goods and machine parts.

Did you know:

The Hudson's Bay Company brought the first blacksmiths to Canada from Britain in the 1670s. The blacksmiths helped build trading posts, and repaired goods and machinery.

Becoming a Blacksmith

Blacksmiths were very important to Canada's pioneers. The blacksmith repaired wagon wheels, made tools such as saws and hammers, and repaired broken tools. These jobs required a great deal of physical strength hauling and hammering the metal pieces. It took a great deal of training to learn how to perform each task. A blacksmith was called a "smith." It was impossible for the blacksmith to make large items without help. **Apprentices** called strikers worked with the blacksmith. A smith stood on one side of an **anvil**, and the striker faced him on the other. The smith pulled the iron out of the fire, and the striker pounded it with the hammer. Many smiths also hired one or two young boys to help in the shop. These boys fanned the fire, ran errands, and swept the shop. These boys often worked to become strikers and smiths themselves.

Each blacksmith made tools in their own special style, known as their signature. People in town could tell which blacksmith made an item by looking at how it was made.

6

Young men who wanted to become blacksmiths were taught blacksmithing, math, reading, and writing.

Did you know:

Many pioneer blacksmiths learned the trade from their fathers. By age 14, many young people were apprenticing. The young people had to work as an apprentice with a blacksmith for at least three years.

First-hand account:

In 1839, poet Henry Wadsworth Longfellow captured the spirit of the blacksmith in his poem "The Village Blacksmith."

Week in, week out, from morn
    till night,
You can hear his **bellows** blow
You can hear him swing his
    heavy sledge
With measured beat and slow....

The Blacksmith's Shop

Most pioneer communities included a blacksmith shop, or "smithy." It was quite often found near the stables. This is because, for many blacksmiths, much of their time was spent shoeing horses.

Blacksmith shops were small, very hot, and often noisy. They housed the smith's fire and various tools needed to do any job. The forge, made of a brick chimney and hearth, or fireplace floor, took up most of the area inside the smithy. Sometimes the forge was outside. The brick that made up the forge's hearth extended to create a table. There, the blacksmith could place finished work to cool. The table also held the iron pieces ready to be put in the fire. Close by was a wooden crane. This pulley system helped blacksmiths lift and move heavy iron pieces in and out of the fire. Even with this help, blacksmithing was an exhausting job.

The blacksmith's shop was a popular place for men in small communities to gather. They talked, played games, and had parties at the shop.

Blacksmith shops were often cluttered with tools, scrap iron, and unfinished projects. However, most blacksmiths had a special area for shoeing horses where the horses would not be upset by loud noises.

Did you know:

The last name "Smith" is common in Canada. People with the name most likely had an **ancestor** who was a blacksmith. The large number of "Smiths" shows how many people once practised this trade.

First-hand account:

Most blacksmith shops had only one or two windows. One pioneer remembers the darkness of the smithy.

The smithy deliberately restricted the amount of light in order to see the glowing colours of the heated metal more clearly in the semi-darkness; this was a crucial means of determining the appropriate temperatures for forging.

Shaping Iron

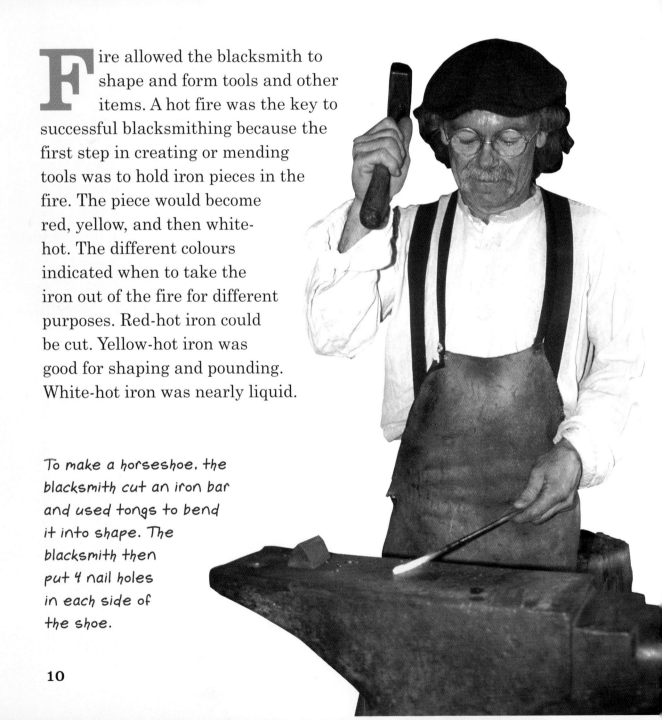

Fire allowed the blacksmith to shape and form tools and other items. A hot fire was the key to successful blacksmithing because the first step in creating or mending tools was to hold iron pieces in the fire. The piece would become red, yellow, and then white-hot. The different colours indicated when to take the iron out of the fire for different purposes. Red-hot iron could be cut. Yellow-hot iron was good for shaping and pounding. White-hot iron was nearly liquid.

To make a horseshoe, the blacksmith cut an iron bar and used tongs to bend it into shape. The blacksmith then put 4 nail holes in each side of the shoe.

Blacksmiths reused most items that came into the shop. For example, they melted down old horseshoes to reshape into new ones.

Once the iron was hot enough, the smith removed it from the fire and used hammers to pound it into the desired shape. Blacksmiths pounded out chains, cowbells, hinges, and **ploughshares**. If the piece cooled, the iron was reheated in the hot fire so that it could be further shaped. When the iron was shaped, the smith dipped the piece in a large tub of water to cool it.

Did you know:

To bring the fire to the right temperature, smiths and their apprentices used bellows to pump air on the fire. Bellows helped give the blacksmith some control over the fire. In the late 1800s, a rotary fan replaced bellows in many shops.

First-hand account:

After 1870, blacksmiths had to compete with factories making iron goods. One blacksmith remembers the difficulties blacksmiths faced in the 1880s.

Blacksmithing is getting Run down to nothing. There is large Factories getting up all over the Country... run by machinery where they do nothing but Wagons and sleighs and sell them all over the Country Cheaper than we can make them.

Tools of the Blacksmith

Blacksmiths valued their tools. Tools were never thrown out, even if they were broken. If tools could not be fixed, smiths melted the iron to make other items. Although the blacksmith's tools have changed over time, they remain important to blacksmithing.

Anvil

The anvil was one of the pioneer blacksmith's most important and heaviest tools. Some anvils weighed more than 135 kilograms. The anvil was placed in the smithy so that it was both close to the fire and always within arms' reach. This way, iron could be put in the fire and retrieved quickly and easily. Most pounding was done on the anvil's smooth, flat, hard top. A cone-shaped spike helped the smith pound rounded iron pieces. The rest of the anvil's top was used as a table. One side of the anvil had two holes that the smith used to punch holes through iron.

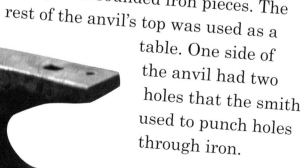

Hammers

Blacksmiths used large and small hammers to pound hot pieces of iron into shape. Some hammers were used lightly for minor shaping and pounding. Others were brought down on metal pieces with great force. The blacksmith's hammers commonly weighed about 1 kilogram.

Tongs and Vises

The iron pieces a blacksmith worked with were extremely hot. Even wearing gloves, a blacksmith could not hold the hot iron. The smith used tongs in various sizes and shapes to safely grip and carry hot pieces of metal. Smiths also used vises to hold iron pieces. Vises were used during the final stages of the job—mostly for polishing and filing.

A Day in the Life

Blacksmiths were usually very busy. They worked steadily all day long. A smith only stopped pounding for as long as it took to heat the iron and cool it in water. All day, the blacksmith and his apprentices stood in the hot shop. They swung heavy hammers and hauled heavy pieces of iron. A typical day for the Canadian pioneer blacksmith may have been like this.

6:00 a.m.

First thing in the morning, often before the sun rose, the smithy's fire had to be stoked. This means the smith had to stir and add fuel to the fire to make it burn hotter. Smiths used charcoal in their fires because charcoal did not create smoke when it burned. Charcoal also burned hotter than other forms of fuel. Once the fire was ready, the blacksmith could begin the day's projects.

7:00 a.m.

Sometimes the smith had customers waiting for him when he opened his shop. If no one was waiting, the smith could begin his day by forging hinges and nails, making horseshoes, and crafting tools. The smith tried to have extras so that customers did not have to wait for the smith to make new ones. Even in the early morning, the sound of tapping and banging from the blacksmith and striker could be heard for miles.

10:00 a.m.

By ten o'clock, the noise from the smithy had drawn a number of townspeople and farmers who had come to town. They brought their broken wheels and carts for the smith to fix. They understood that they would often have to wait for the blacksmith. The smith and striker could not put their hammers down until forging was complete. If a smith or striker stopped working before a project was completed, the iron would be ruined. The waiting townspeople took advantage of this time to chat with each other about politics and the weather.

noon

Around noon, the smith and striker took a short break to eat lunch. If they were in the middle of a project, their hunger had to wait. The smith and striker ate very quickly. If it was a slow day, they enjoyed a one-hour break. Most times, they went back to work within half an hour.

4:00 p.m.

By four o'clock, school was finished for the day. The sound of the blacksmith at work often drew children from around the town. They loved to watch smiths create hooks, nails, and tools from iron.

6:00 p.m.

At the end of the day, about six o'clock, the blacksmith's assistant stoked the fire one last time. They left the fire burning overnight. A bucket of ashes was often scattered over the fire to trap the heat overnight. In the morning, it took the blacksmith only a few minutes to get the fire back to working temperature.

The Blacksmith's Customers

Nearly all Canadian pioneers visited the blacksmith shop at one time or another. Some farmers were able to forge their own nails and hinges. However, they brought larger and more difficult projects into town to the blacksmith. Smiths pounded out chains, cowbells, and ploughshares while the farmers went about their other business in town.

Early blacksmiths spent most of their time shoeing horses. This was a difficult job because the horse had to be kept calm while putting the shoes on. Loud noises frighten horses.

One young Canadian pioneer remembers watching the blacksmith at work.

The horse shoe was held in the hot coals of the forge. When it was red hot, it was pounded on the anvil and then cooled in water. The steam would be all over. The shoe was then fitted on the horse. After this was done a few times and the right fit achieved, it would be nailed on to the horse's hoof, the nails clipped off and then rasped or smoothed off around the horse's hoof.

Did you know:

Account books show that typical blacksmiths spent 40 percent of their time shoeing horses. Fixing and creating farm tools accounted for 20 percent of their time, and fixing wagons and sleighs took about 14 percent of their time.

Some townspeople came to the blacksmith to have their horses shod. Blacksmiths who specialized in shoeing horses were called farriers. They made shoes to fit a specific hoof on a specific horse. To save time, sometimes farriers made horseshoes that could be reshaped to fit specific horses. Farriers shaped and pounded iron rods to make horseshoes. Then they nailed the new shoes onto the horse's hoofs.

The Blacksmith in the Community

The blacksmith was an important person in Canadian pioneer communities. The early settlers relied on the blacksmith to provide them with tools. The blacksmith also filled other roles. In some early communities, the blacksmith was also the banker, doctor, and **veterinarian**. Sometimes a blacksmith lent money—and charged interest—to other citizens. Sometimes the blacksmith was paid with grain, meat, and vegetables. If the smith could not use all of these products, they would be sold.

Blacksmiths were sometimes paid with goods such as chickens instead of cash. They kept a few chickens for eggs and meat, then sold the rest to their customers.

First-hand account:

A pioneer shares the experience of watching the blacksmith pull teeth.

Of course when using such clumsy tools, mistakes were inevitable, and once when he had pulled a tooth pointed out by his agonized patient as the source of his trouble, it was after the operation discovered that [he had] pulled a wrong tooth. Second attempt corrected the mistake. The gap in the patient's mouth became wider than originally planned, but it was a small matter.

Did you know:

Early blacksmiths specialized in one kind of iron work, such as creating hinges or making saws. In the mid-1800s, blacksmiths who did many kinds of work replaced those who specialized in specific tasks.

The smith was often the only person in Canada's early communities with the tools to pull teeth. People with toothaches went to the blacksmith to have painful teeth removed. During the nineteenth century, many people believed diseased blood had to be removed from a sick person's body before they would get well. Blacksmiths had the necessary tools to remove diseased blood through a process known as "bleeding." Smiths often performed this operation on animals as well.

Blacksmiths Past and Present

By the turn of the twentieth century, blacksmithing was becoming **obsolete**. By the mid-twentieth century, there were very few blacksmiths. Technology and factories had replaced the pioneer blacksmith's craft. It was less expensive to buy new items than it was to repair old or broken ones. It seemed the art would be lost forever.

Competition

Modern blacksmiths can test their skills at the World Championship Blacksmiths' Competition. This event is held every year at the Calgary Exhibition and Stampede in Calgary, Alberta. Blacksmiths from around the world compete at forging, shoeing, and creative metalwork.

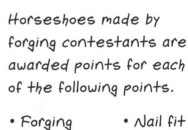

Modern blacksmiths use traditional methods to forge items.

Horseshoes made by forging contestants are awarded points for each of the following points.

- Forging
- Nail placement
- Size
- Nail fit
- Level
- Finish

Then

Early Blacksmith

- An important person in pioneer towns
- Created everything from raw materials
- Made own tools
- Provided a good and steady living

- Look at the metal's colour to determine its readiness for different processes
- Use anvil and hammer
- Work spaces often small and dark
- Requires strength to forge and pound metals

Now

Today's Blacksmith

- Often done as a hobby
- Materials often created in bulk in factories
- Tools bought at stores
- Use power tools and blowers
- Some smiths use gas forges rather than charcoal fires

DIAGRAM

Working with metal in the pioneer days was very different from modern times. The diagram on the left compares these differences and similarities. Copy the diagram in your notebook. Try to think of other similarities and differences to add to your diagram.

As you can see from the diagram, blacksmiths today have some things in common with blacksmiths more than 100 years ago.

Preserving the Past

In the 1970s, more people became interested in blacksmithing. Most of this new interest in the trade came from hobby blacksmiths rather than career blacksmiths. Many of these people learned the old ways of forging. Historical societies have also done their part to protect the ways of the pioneer blacksmith. Across the country, blacksmithing shops have been preserved to show what life was like more than a century ago. Some old shops were made into museums. Others are still used to demonstrate the techniques and tools of these craftsmen. Here are a few examples of these locations.

1 **Barr & Combs Blacksmith Shop**
Fort Steele Historical Town, Fort Steele, BC

2 **Flett's Blacksmith**
Heritage Park Historical Village, Calgary, AB

3 **The Blacksmith Shop**
Melfort and District Museum, Melfort, SK

4 **The Blacksmith Shop**
Manitoba Agricultural Museum, Austin, MB

5 **Blacksmith Shop**
Upper Canada Village, Morrisburg, ON

6 **Suderman Barn and Blacksmith Shop**
Backus Heritage Village, Port Rowan, ON

7 **The Forge à Pique-Assaut**
Ornamental Blacksmith Museum, Saint-Laurent, Île d'Orléans, QB

8 **Blacksmith Shop**
Central New Brunswick Woodmen's Museum, Boiestown, NB

9 **Milton Blacksmith Shop Museum**
Milton Heritage Society, Liverpool, NS

10 **Blacksmith Shop**
Alberton Museum, Alberton, PEI

11 **Green Family Forge**
Blacksmith Museum, Trinity, NL

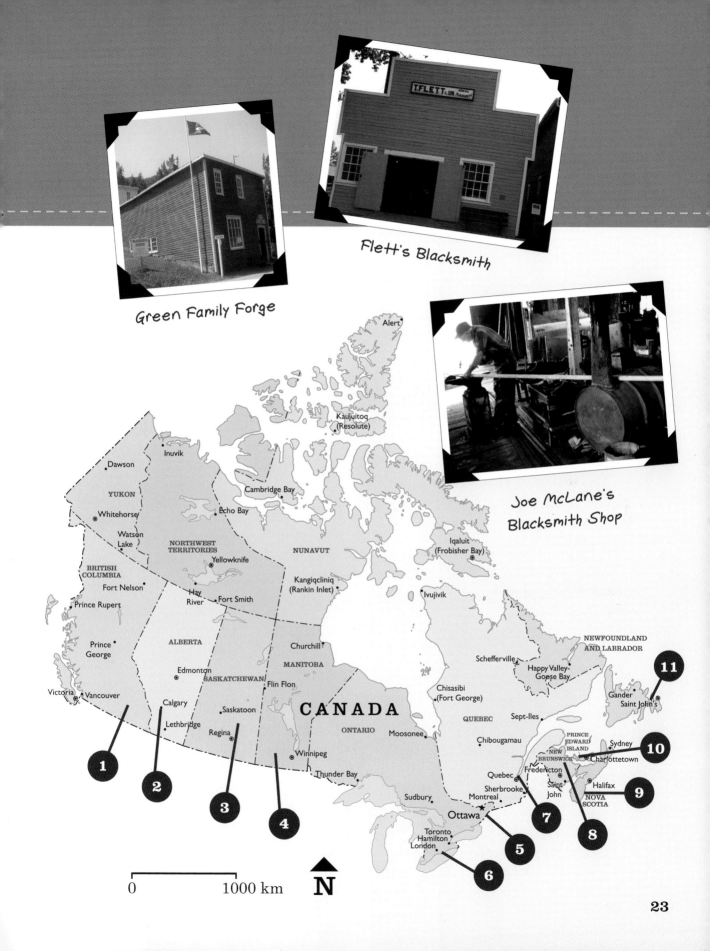

Green Family Forge

Flett's Blacksmith

Joe McLane's
Blacksmith Shop

Alert

Kaujuitoq
(Resolute)

Inuvik

Dawson

YUKON

Whitehorse

Watson
Lake

Cambridge Bay

Echo Bay

NORTHWEST
TERRITORIES

Yellowknife

NUNAVUT

BRITISH
COLUMBIA

Fort Nelson

Hay
River

Fort Smith

Kangiqcliniq
(Rankin Inlet)

Iqaluit
(Frobisher Bay)

Prince Rupert

Ivujivik

Prince
George

ALBERTA

Edmonton

Churchill

MANITOBA

NEWFOUNDLAND
AND LABRADOR

Schefferville

Happy Valley-
Goose Bay

Gander

11

Victoria

Vancouver

Calgary

Saskatoon

SASKATCHEWAN

Flin Flon

Chisasibi
(Fort George)

Saint John's

Lethbridge

Regina

CANADA

ONTARIO

Winnipeg

QUEBEC

Sept-Iles

Chibougamau

PRINCE
EDWARD
ISLAND

Sydney

10

1

2

3

4

Thunder Bay

Moosonee

Quebec

Sherbrooke

NEW
BRUNSWICK

Fredericton

Charlottetown

Sudbury

Montreal

Saint
John

Halifax

9

NOVA
SCOTIA

Ottawa

7

8

Toronto
Hamilton
London

5

6

0   1000 km

N

23

Glossary

Agonized: suffered extreme pain

Ancestor: a person from whom one is descended, such as a parent or grandparent

Anvil: an iron block on which smiths hammer metal

Apprentices: people learning a craft on-the-job from a professional

Bellows: devices that are expanded and flattened to create and expel air

Crucial: very important

Inevitable: unavoidable; certain to happen

Obsolete: out of date; no longer used

Ploughshares: parts of ploughs that cut soil

Veterinarian: animal doctor

Index